Wisdom Is Where You Find It
or Where It Finds You

Wisdom Is Where You Find It
or Where It Finds You

JAMES I. WARREN

UPPER
ROOM BOOKS
NASHVILLE

Cover Art Direction: Michele Wetherbee
Cover Design: Marc Tedeschi
Interior Design and Layout: Cindy Helms
Interior Line Art: Marjorie Warren
First Printing: April 1997 (5)

The Upper Room Web Site: http://www.upperroom.org

Library of Congress Cataloging-in-Publication Data

Warren, James I.
        Wisdom is where you find it or where it finds
    you/James I. Warren
            p.cm.
        ISBN 0-8358-0801-7 (pbk.)
        1. Christian life. 2. Warren, James I. I. Title
BV4501.2.W3755   1997
248.4--dc21   97-896
                                                      CIP
Printed in the United States of America

*T*o Andrew, Hailey, Jim IV, Hannah, and all who seek sweetness and light.

Contents

Preface

She ticked me off. Madeleine L'Engle. The Intentional Growth Center, where I work, had engaged her for four days of lectures and discussions, paying her a hefty honorarium. While introducing Madeleine I put in a plug for the center. I was shocked when she began by saying, "Well, I don't know about you, but most of my growth has been *unintentional.*" Her audience of writers and would-be writers chuckled, and she took her discourse in another direction. I was not amused. With a quip, she had dismissed something dear to my heart. Indeed, I felt betrayed.

While Madeleine continued talking, my mind would not let go of her challenge. To what extent was her remark true? How much of my own personal, professional, and spiritual growth had come through intentionality and discipline? How much, on the other hand, had come unplanned and unexpected—even unrecognized at the time?

For months, I pondered this riddle. The scope of my

quest broadened. What persons and what events had created a fertile environment for my self-discovery? instructed me in human nature and human potential? given rise to my values and goals? shaped my worldview?

This book is the product of my musings. It is a way for me to express my appreciation for instructors and mentors in formal settings—for example, my fifty years' involvement with educational institutions. (This enormous investment may have triggered my instant resentment toward Madeleine.) It is, at the same time, a celebration of unlikely and unsolicited sources of wisdom; I recognize that many "ordinary" people impacted my life.

So, my growth has been both intentional and unintentional. (Once I got beyond being peeved with Madeleine, I heard her saying that is the way it had been with her.) I invite you, as you read this book, to reflect upon the events and persons that have been channels for growth in your life. You may, as I have, grow additionally through such a review, becoming more open to appropriating wisdom from whatever source. I have concluded that wisdom is where you find it—or where it finds you.

Hark! the Herald Angels Come

I had a problem. Two problems, really—one nine years old, the other six. Their names were Derek and Allison, and they needed a home at Christmas, and that home was going to be mine if Marjorie had her way. I protested against this invasion by strangers, bolstered by wavering support from Heather, Jimmy, and Hilary.

On earlier occasions, I had spoken casually to Derek and Allison, and I had exchanged pleasantries with their parents, who were originally from England and had more recently served as teaching missionaries in Africa. Now they were on a study sabbatical at Scarritt Graduate School, where I was a professor. True to the British tradition, they were unassuming and self-reliant. But then, in late November, the wife and mother became seriously ill. Surgery was recommended, but the family's meager resources couldn't afford an expensive operation and long hospital stay. Fortunately a surgeon in Louisiana volunteered, and a local church agreed to pick up the hospital bill. A major hitch remained—what to do with the children?

Sure we had room, Marjorie asserted. Allison could bunk in with our two girls, and Derek with Jimmy. Bathrooms would be taxed and there would be a squeeze at the dinner table, but we would manage. I and the children didn't think so. I had been anticipating the holidays as an opportunity for intimacy with my family and respite from my job with the college and from serving my little church (a vacation from being "nice"). But my righteous wife prevailed and, three weeks before Christmas, Derek and Allison moved in for a month's stay.

They were model children and instantly I fell in love with them. Derek was well mannered, and oh, so dedicated to his little sister. A surrogate parent, he got Allison ready for bed, school, and church. Away from the house he protected and comforted her. He showed his gratitude to us by insisting on doing chores.

Marjorie and I had saved for Christmas and had already bought some of the big-ticket items that our children wanted or needed. Santa was really going to please them! But what about Derek and Allison? We had very little discretionary money. From conversations, we picked up Derek's desire, above anything else in the world, for a guitar. After all, he was living in Nashville, "Music City,

USA," and he had shown an aptitude for music. As for Allison, she loved our girls' dolls and wanted one of her own. We talked with our children and were delighted when they expressed a desire to pare their want-lists in order to share with Derek and Allison. But while we could handle the expense of a nice doll, a decent guitar seemed beyond our means.

To the rescue came my little church, Pegram United Methodist Church, which I served as part-time pastor and what I always considered one of the greatest churches in Christendom. The Pegram community was situated about fifteen miles outside of Nashville, and the church's one hundred members were mostly working class; indeed, some were working two jobs to make ends meet. But these good people's hearts were bigger than their pocketbooks, and they reached deep to see that "these little angels" had a proper Christmas. They had the kids into their homes and invited them to community celebrations, often slipping them tokens of their affection. An example was Grover Anderson, a legend for his Christmas trees decorated with silver dollars. Each child that visited him, including Derek and Allison, was invited to remove one of the coins for their use.

The elusive guitar? Rachael and Bill Herbert heard about the wish (which Derek never would have expressed as a request) and called us. "Buy him a nice guitar and send the bill to us."

Christmas morning, all five kids awakened early and hurried us into the den to see what miracles Santa had accomplished. As I recall, our three were satisfied with their abbreviated gifts. Allison was overjoyed with her doll, which she mommied all day. And Derek, in great disbelief, spotted the guitar and repeated over and over, "Is it really mine?"

I have long since forgotten the presents that our own family received; I'm sure they were nice. But we had received something else that was marvelous and wonderful, those little herald angels who brought us tidings of great joy. They blessed our home and our church. In their innocence, they reminded us of baby Jesus. That season, not only did we feel a closeness of family, but also the warmth of community.

Derek and Allison brought alive for me the verse in Hebrews 13:2: "Do not neglect to show hospitality to strangers, for by doing that some have entertained angels without knowing it."

Trying to Pay off the Good Samaritan

*F*rom Cambuslang to Glasgow University is twelve miles—and a long twelve miles it can be! Let me tell you (in a round-about way) how far.

While a student of the university and Trinity College, I lived in MacBrayne Hall with a cosmopolitan community of students. John McGufog, from Largs, would later serve as best man at my wedding. Ben Compani, an Irani Muslim, shared with me his concerns about dietary laws. Jack Abraham, from London, told me how his parents had escaped the holocaust in Germany. Always, just down the hall, was a scholar in some specialty, ready to enlighten me or help with an academic problem. A bonus of learning came when the Reverend Donald McDonald became ill and I assisted him in his pastorate of Trinity Church of Scotland. Add the faculty, and I would say wisdom was rampant.

But while intellectual exercises filled my mind, romantic thoughts filled my heart, for in the village of

Cambuslang I discovered and wooed (and later wed) lovely Marjorie Logie. During the courtship, as we Americans say, I burned up the road between the university and Cambuslang.

One night, following a delightful visit with Marjorie and her family and friends, I said goodnight and walked a mile to the bus stop. To my despair, I found that I had missed the last conveyance to the city. I didn't want to return to Marjorie's home and perhaps wake up her parents, so I began hiking the twelve miles to my lodging, all the while hoping that a vacant taxi might happen along.

Having trekked a mile without significant headway, I was cheered by the sound of a slowing car. The driver called out, "Can I give you a lift, son?" You bet. As we motored along, he recounted occasions when he had found himself stranded, and my comments revealed me to be an American. We shifted to comparing, in a studiedly genteel way, characteristics of my land and his. Time passed quickly, and as we neared the central city, his declared destination, I told him that once we were in town, I would be able to catch a cab to my residence. No trouble, he would drive me to MacBrayne Hall. And he did.

I thanked him profusely, but then I wondered— maybe a thank-you wasn't what he had in mind. Unsettled, I slipped a bill out of my wallet and extended it to him. "I would have spent this much on cab fare," I explained.

The driver brushed away my money and his tone turned hard. "That's the trouble with you ruddy Yanks. You think you can buy anything and everything." And he motored away.

I was humiliated. And it wasn't until I hit the sack that I allowed myself a chuckle over the iconoclastic Scot who was neither penny-pinching nor money-grabbing. But his lesson has stuck with me.

We Americans (and maybe we aren't all that peculiar) find it diffucult to accept a gift, a favor, a compliment. After all, we are conditioned to be ashamed of a handout; we're supposed to earn our way! As children, we perform like trained puppies to earn a pat on the head. In school, we go for the grade and forfeit the joy of learning. At home, to sustain the affection of a spouse we stack the folded laundry so it can be seen and appreciated rather than put it away. No wonder that when a generous act befalls us, we blush and stammer and say, "You shouldn't have" or "My treat next time!"

The Tower of Babel is a monument to people who didn't appreciate their blessings. They plotted to storm heaven and commandeer—*what*? Such gifts as were already theirs. They should have stayed on the ground and said "Thank you, Lord."

Granted, some people find it all too easy to accept the products of somebody else's labors, and that can be evil.

But arrogance is as sinful as sloth because it presumes that we are too smart, too rich, too powerful to need other people and their gifts.

Generosity and grace go hand in hand. Generosity is giving freely and without counting the cost. Graceful acceptance is accepting freely without embarrassment or fear of being in the donor's debt. Usually, giver and beneficiary are served best by a simple "thank-you."

Camelot and the Gothic Principle

*L*ife in the Middle Ages was notoriously rude and barbarous; yet the period gave birth to inspiring Gothic architecture, which, in receptive people, causes the spirit to soar. Howard Thurman borrows from this symbolism in the concept that he calls the "gothic principle." He convincingly argues that the human spirit can never be earthbound; no matter how crushing the circumstances, the soul will aspire to and strive for fulfillment. That's the "gothic principle."

In the challenging treatise *Deep River: The Negro Spiritual Speaks of Life and Death*, Thurman exhibits spirituals to exemplify the indomitability of the human spirit. Slaves, who originated these traditional songs, were assaulted by drudgery, brutality, and derision. Often they were considered little more than animals. Yet, they eloquently sang of hope—hope for deliverance, freedom, and justice.

One of Thurman's samples is "There Is a Balm in Gilead." A place celebrated for healing, Gilead was the Mayo Clinic of the ancient world. The prophet Jeremiah, grieving for his evil generation, refers to this celebrity when he rhetorically asks, "Is there no balm in Gilead? Is there no physician there?" (Jeremiah 8:22). The presumed answer is no. But in the spiritual the singers affirm that, indeed, "There is a balm in Gilead, to make the wounded whole; there is a balm in Gilead, to heal the sin-sick soul." Thurman says the singers straightened the question mark into an exclamation point!

The Gothic cathedral, firmly planted on the ground, sends its ceiling vaulting, and the beholder looks upward both spatially and spiritually. Speaking to our spiritual dimension, Jean-Paul Sartre, employing existential language, says the human being is a *no-thing*—having essence beyond the realm of things. Our spirit resides in a *there* that is beyond finger-pointing capability. Similarly, Saint Augustine, using phenomenological concepts, observes that persons—spiritual and transcendent—can never be fulfilled by possessions and by activities, whether tawdry (sexual conquests) or noble (giving to the poor). We experience unease even while we presume ourselves "secure." ("Thou hast made us for Thyself, and our hearts are restless till they rest in Thee." Augustine) The human spirit, seemingly held down by earthly woes, breaks loose and rises to search for the *more* and the *ought-to-be*; indeed, the essence of humankind is to transcend limits.

Thoughts on transcendence are not peculiar to saints and mystics, philosophers, and theologians. Songwriters treat such themes eloquently. Nearly every musical has at least one haunting song of aspiration. Lerner and Loewe's 1960 musical *Camelot* chronicles King Arthur's attempts to establish a chivalrous realm. He aspires to a sunny, happy place, but as the play's acting and singing progress, we become aware that Arthur's hopes are not so much located by geography as by the ideals of "more" and "ought-to-be." Camelot is not so much a place that "once was" as it is a way of life that "ought-to-be." It is a representation of aspiring for the "more" of a "once and future" ideal. In the celebrated reprise, which the king sings as he enters his last battle, Arthur charges his squire to let it not be forgotten that there was a Camelot. But, as he sings, we do more than remember; we know that there should be a Camelot and that we ourselves are being charged to bring it into being.

Graduating classes latch onto "You'll Never Walk Alone" from *Carousel* because its unapologetic sentiment exhorts them to walk on with hope in their hearts and with the assurance that they will not be alone. Richard Rodgers using a simple, stair-step device that is imperceptible to most listeners, heightens the mood of Oscar Hammerstein's lyrics by raising the interior notes of chords just a half tone. In the phrase "Walk on, walk on," he elevates the G to a G-sharp, brightening both the chord and the listener's resolve. Likewise, in *The Sound of Music* Hammerstein inspires us to climb every mountain, while Rodgers boosts our spirits with a determined tempo that is accentuated with chordal resolutions.

In *Man of La Mancha* Don Quixote travels the countryside attempting to right wrongs (often in foolish ways) simply because there is a soul of nobility within the frail frame of this out-of-sync old knight. His motley followers also find meaning in the pursuit of righteous causes. Their heroic quest for justice and beauty finds its most eloquent expression in the song "The Impossible Dream." Here Don Quixote avers that, scorn and scars suffered by questers notwithstanding, the world is bettered when even one person dares to dream the impossible and reach for the unreachable.

The "gothic principle," by other names, has been promulgated by prophets, poets, scholars, rulers, and slaves. It is embodied in quiet waiting and tumultuous rebellion. It is the yeast of personal struggles and growth. It straightens question marks into exclamation points.

Although I never met Thurman, Sartre, Augustine, or Cervantes, I sometimes have the feeling, while reading their works, that I am conversing with old friends. I respond to their interpretations of the "gothic principle" with *How true!* or *Hmm, I wonder about that.* And, I thank them for reminding me that because we are who we are our reach must exceed our grasp.

The Preacher
Provokes an "Uh-oh!"

When we go to church, we optimistically assume that the minister has carefully chosen his text and theme, has studied and prayed, and has rehearsed his message. We expect a lot from the preacher; unfortunately, we don't expect much from the congregation. Wisdom from the preacher? Yes. From his listeners? Nah.

For Ministers' Week in Raleigh, North Carolina, several hundred pastors had assembled for worship, Bible study, and workshops. A seminary professor was the main speaker. It was preaching in the grand tradition. He dramatically related episodes in the David and Jonathan chronicles and interspersed the stories with illustrations of friendship from his own experiences.

The preacher was dynamic, entertaining, and honest. The congregation was attentive; indeed, several listeners down front were really "into" these sessions, first with an affirming nod, then "Amen," "That's right," and "Un-huh."

One dialogue went like this:

"Everybody needs a friend like Jonathan."

"That's right!"

"We all need somebody we can count on."

"Amen!"

"Somebody we can tell our joys, sorrows, problems."

"Un-huh."

"I'm thankful I have such a friend."

"Yes!"

"I can tell her anything, no matter how bad or how silly, and I know she will listen, still love me, remain my friend."

"That's good."

"And she's not my wife."

"Uh-oh!"

This was the most sincere congregational response I have ever heard. The brother in the pew was listening, appropriating, and sharing feedback directly from his mind and heart. He had liked what he was hearing—and then the preacher threw him a curve. The listener's one-word response spoke volumes.

"Uh-oh" may have expressed surprise. "You mean you're close to a woman not your wife!"

Or perplexity. "I'm not too sure about this. I'll have to think about it."

It may have been a warning, "Look out, you may be

headed for trouble."

Or it could have been an invitation. "Don't leave me hanging. Talk to me further about this."

Surprise is wise, for it grabs one's audience. ("And she isn't my wife.") Oh, for a sense of wonder! My little grandson encountered a duck for the first time. A dog ran up and immediately the duck took to the air. Andrew's open-mouthed amazement was priceless. A walking creature can fly? Preposterous!

In our practice of scientific rationality, we have caused our language to become trite, our routines banal, our passions lukewarm, our commitments conditional. Rather than reach on tiptoe, we stand flatfooted. The most persistent heresy of the Christian faith is gnosticism, which, simply stated, is the desire to substitute knowledge for faith. We're not supposed to understand everything. In *The Christian Agnostic* Leslie D. Weatherhead acknowledged that lives may need mental boxes labeled "awaiting further light."

We need more uh-ohs in our worship and in our lives. Such expressions show that we are alive and searching. In contrast a posture of knowing it all undercuts faith and stagnates living.

"Uh-oh!" and "Amen!"

Learning the Arithmetic of Love

*E*very Sunday morning, my sister, Betty, and I awakened early and raced down the driveway to fetch the paper. Before we were back in the house, we had extracted that delight of delights, the comics section. We leapt into our parents' bed demanding, "Read us the funny papers!" We were impatient to see what hilarious prank the Katzenjammer Kids had pulled on the Captain. Would Jiggs circumvent Maggie's tyranny and enjoy his corned beef and cabbage? And we anticipated that Joe Palooka and Smiling Jack would triumph, but how?

Dad and Mother exchanged pained looks; then, with a sigh, one of them began reading the mysterious balloons, pointing to the pictures so that we could keep up with the action. We welcomed their exaggerated interjections of "Ho-ho!" and "My, my!" as part of the fiction. When the last panel had been dramatized, we were dejected—our parents relieved. Strange creatures, adults.

It was in these Sunday morning sessions that I learned the power of words, the competitiveness and incongruities of life, and the joy of unbridled laughter. And I still love the funnies. I marvel at Mary Worth's inexhaustible supply of advice. I suffer along with Cathy over her diet, wardrobe, and fractured relationships. In *Peanuts*, I see reflections of myself and handily match friends with Charlie Brown, Lucy, or Snoopy.

Often when I'm immersed in the comics, a shaft of wisdom shines through the humor. Take, for example, Hagar the Horrible, an overweight Norse warrior with a penchant for bravado and a zest for plunder, ale, and life. Ostensibly, he dominates his wife, Helga, but in truth she's stronger, smarter, and more insightful.

In one strip, Helga surprises Hagar by saying she does not wish to be called his "other half." When Hagar asks why, she surprises him and us by answering, "I want to be fifty-one percent."

How human! We're not satisfied for our basketball team to stand at .500. We must have a winning season. We interrupt conversations because we presume we have a better idea. We swerve around the guy in front of us because our destination seems more important. When we show off our new car, we boast that it was a "steal"—clever us, we outfoxed the salesperson. The world revolves around us, our town, our nation. Even in our prayers, we want more than our fair share: "O Lord, bless me and my wife and our son, John, and his wife—us four and no more."

It sounds idealistic but the saying "It is more blessed to give than to receive" is right. The person who gives more gets more. The giver gains an inner glow, a sense of importance and fulfillment. To paraphrase scripture, "Whosoever among you would like a greater than fifty percent slice of life's pie, let him or her invest more than fifty percent in the kitchen" (Mark 10:4). Marriages based on the fifty percent standard lack the vitality and durability of spontaneously generous unions in which each mate goes the extra mile simply because he or she loves the other person without measure. The arithmetic of relationships is tricky: Fifty percent plus fifty percent doesn't always add up to one hundred percent.

I'm not suggesting that a person should be a doormat; everyone is entitled to privacy, relaxation, a sense of dignity, and the satisfaction of being appreciated. But if you're always thinking and acting like an accountant, you won't be sufficiently relaxed to relish any relationship.

Helga, in spite of her usual wisdom, is cheating herself when she demands fifty-one percent. She simply doesn't understand the arithmetic of love.

A Tree as Lovely
as a Poem

*I*t was a church made in heaven although it was built just outside Nashville. I considered myself blessed to be a part of it.

The building, only two years old, was attractive, comfortable, and neatly maintained. The grounds were spectacular, planted and groomed by volunteers. We had the use of a community house and playing fields nearby.

The most beautiful part was the people, all one hundred of them. As pastor, I was part time, so in large measure the congregation had to be the salt—and the pepper. They unstintingly invested their time, energy, prayers, and money. They shared their faith by precept and example, visited the sick, comforted the bereaved, encouraged the weak, and punched up the lax. The choir—our untrained voices—made a joyful noise to the Lord. A rarity among churches, two avuncular gentlemen minded the nursery during worship. They said they couldn't tear themselves away from the little ones, half of which were their grandchildren, but I accused them of skipping out on my sermons.

Loyalty! I was having difficulty with the president of the college where I taught, and one Wednesday night I shared my distress during our weekly Bible study and sharing session. We prayed that the rift would dissolve. What followed was perhaps the most generous offer of assistance I ever received. A parishioner, whose vocabulary came straight off his riverboat, sidled up to me and said, "Preacher, that #*+=@! needs a talking-to that wouldn't be appropriate for you to do, so I'm gonna drive into Nashville and tell the *&$#*@ off!" I thanked him but said I favored a milder approach.

Because attendance at worship was small (seventy on average) and we were closely knit, I could comfortably be innovative. Once I preached on "He is like a tree planted by streams of water, that yields its fruit in its season." I compared the parts of a tree—roots, trunk, foliage, fruit—to our human condition. Nothing novel about that. But then I distributed paper and crayons to the congregation and asked them to draw and color two pictures. First, to portray their present-day selves as a tree, and then to depict the kind of tree into which they might be transmuted by the grace of God.

As I had anticipated, most of the "now" self-portraits

were scraggly, while the wishful images were strong and productive, even towering.

One lady who was concerned about her wrinkles drew a prune tree. (Of course, there is no such thing as a *prune tree*. Prunes, everybody knows, come from plums, which grow on plum trees.) Her "after" image was a peach tree, with luscious fruit "as smooth as a peach."

The artists, one at a time, were invited to bring their sketches to the chancel and explain them, and to share with their fellow members the blessings, misgivings, yearnings, and resolves that prompted their interpretations. The presentations and responses were so captivating that the exchanges spilled beyond the benediction.

I thought my own art was acceptable, if obvious. "Now I'm a pretty good guy (average fruit tree) but with God's help I'm going to become a Christian overflowing with love" (a tree groaning with fruit).

The most compelling pictures were done by two young girls. One aspired to be a flowering dogwood that afforded a nesting site for a family of birds. The other projected herself as a giant oak with sturdy, spreading branches. One limb supported a rope swing for children to enjoy. What wonderful visions—lives providing security and joy. Now, many years later, I hope that the lives of these young women are as beautiful and generous as they, while youngsters, envisioned them.

You Are What You Sing

Nowadays, "background" or "elevator" music surrounds me without penetrating my consciousness; but in my earlier years (as a schoolboy, college student, and suitor), I focused on music. Thanks to radio, music permeated my life and certain songs were central in it. Back then, families bonded as they gathered around the radio to catch national and world news, fascinated by the speed with which it was transmitted. And entertainment! You could walk down the street at 6:30 p.m. and hardly miss a line of *Lum and Abner*.

"No television?" youngsters might ask today. It may seem impossible, but there was no television during those days. Radio shaped our hearts and our vocabularies. Someone was as stingy as Jack Benny. A room was as cluttered as Fibber Magee's closet. Fred Allen and his zany friends permitted us to laugh through hard times. We allowed ourselves to be horrified by *Inner Sanctum* from the

moment we heard the eerie creaking of the infamous door. I
rushed home from school Mondays, Wednesdays, and
Fridays to catch the latest episode of *The Lone Ranger.*
When I heard "Hi-ho, Sliver," I felt the mighty stallion's
flesh surge beneath me.

More vitally for me, radio was music. Romantic
songs of fulfilled love and of unrequited love. Songs lifting
up patriotism, valor, ambition, sacrifice. In large degree, we
were what we sang. Did the music shape us, or did we
gravitate towards songs that represented our yearnings?
Either way, there was an undeniable correlation.

My notion of correlating personality and character
with music was corroborated for me during an Elderhostel
course in which I led ninety participants through a review
of their musical pasts.

After surveying the songs that illuminate our
national history, we shifted to our personal lives, and the
session turned into a "testimony meeting." The song "Over
There" memorialized a father who had not come home from
World War I. "When the Lights Go on Again" recalled the
loneliness of a spouse while her mate was in the Pacific
Theater during World War II. "Moments to Remember"
commemorated happy college antics, like tearing the goal
posts down. A trio recreated the wacky "Mairzy Doats" and
confessed that our generation too was loony. A couple
recalled the giddiness they felt (still feel) upon hearing

"People Will Say We're in Love." Our conversations revealed
that music has a mysterious capacity for recreating episodes
in our lives as dramatically as vignettes played out on a
stage.

"Now," I suggested, "tell us what one song, more
than any other, characterizes you?"

There were a few ready answers and a lot of
pondering. A short, peppy woman recited "Five Feet Two,
Eyes of Blue." A genial optimist came up with "Sunshine on
My Shoulders." An introspective lady told us that "What's It
All about, Alfie?" spoke to her continuing quest for meaning
in her life.

What is my own torch song? I second a colleague's
choice, "The Impossible Dream." While still in his teens, he
supported himself by taking odd jobs, all the while staying
in school. He put himself through college and at work rose
through the ranks to become a corporate executive. He
attributed his accomplishments to a childhood longing to
"be somebody," coupled with his seemingly natural ability to
work with people. He encouraged subordinates to be the
best they could be, and their successes boosted his own
career as well as their own.

As I listened to the stories, I was impressed by both
their diversity and universality. Recalling favorite songs
and reflecting on their words and music open doors to the
past, and we can review who we were and examine who we

are. Moreover, noting what songs we currently sing or listen to highlights our enduring values and may remind us of dreams we have not yet fulfilled. Insights and wisdom may be right on the tips of our tongues.

Fanny Crosby's Vibrating Chords

*F*anny Crosby lived for ninety-five years, wrote some 9,000 poems and hymns, and conversed with six presidents. Yet I, as a young man, joined the coterie of "theologically correct" intellectuals who belittled the old lady. We viewed her as a minor poet who gushed sentimental drivel. She was uncritically conservative, we opined, and she oversimplified human problems and solutions. Even biographer Bernard Ruffin found the popular appeal of her songs to be catchy rhythms and flowery phrasing.

We viewed her as a child of her era, the end of the nineteenth century and beginning of the twentieth, a period well known for its sentimental poetry. Her milieu was the Sunday School and the Missionary Society, and her medium was the plinking piano accompanied by untrained voices. So, I reasoned, *how could this relic of unsophisticated times speak to me and my generation, enmeshed as we were in rampant social change and intellectual ferment, adrift on the uncharted seas of situational ethics, and defeated by the seeming impossibility of achieving international peace and justice, not to mention rescuing the planet from environmental degradation?*

While attending an evening church service in spite of (or perhaps because of) a dark mood, a song broke into my heart, bringing solace and hope. *Yes,* I said to myself, *these verses tell it like it is. This is how I feel.* The author was Fanny Crosby.

> Rescue the perishing, care for the dying,
> Snatch them in pity from sin and the grave;
> Weep o'er the erring one, lift up the fallen,
> Tell them of Jesus, the mighty to save.
>
> Down in the human heart, crushed by the tempter,
> Feelings lie buried that grace can restore;
> Touched by a loving heart, wakened by kindness,
> Chords that were broken will vibrate once more.

As a youngster, I had sung "Rescue the Perishing" mechanically; now I was open to its profound statements on the human condition. We are, indeed, erring. Crushed, we fall. But we are not hopelessly depraved. Dormant within us are noble feelings that grace can restore. It is the duty of every Christian to weep over us when we fall, to tell us of Jesus, "the mighty to save," and to offer love and kindness so that healing can take place.

My new appreciation for the hymn prompted me to research Fanny Crosby's life and ministry. She was far from an unthinking Pollyanna. She was blind from childhood, and she wrote "Rescue the Perishing" at bedtime after she had visited an inner city mission in Cincinnati, where she talked with a young man newly arrived from a rural area. He was depressed over his inability to make ends meet; he felt alone and bereft of his sense of integrity and community. It seemed God had forsaken him. Fanny Crosby befriended him, as she did hundreds of down-and-out workers.

I had been so wrong about Frances Jane Crosby. She didn't dash off her poetry during spells of religious ecstasy; they were grounded in the real world. She spent her later years working in missions and prisons. She didn't think salvation was acquired by simply being zapped during an altar call; instead, she believed faith was a journey, and she helped travelers along their way. This sounds like the language we church folk employ today.

I especially like Fanny Crosby's imagery, "Chords that are broken will vibrate once more." A chord is a combination of tones sounded simultaneously, usually with a powerful and harmonious effect. A pianist can create such a chord by causing two or more strings to vibrate at the same time. A blended, creative, and useful life is like a harmonious chord. And you and I can help the discouraged and downfallen to set their life-chords to vibrating once more by encouraging them and supporting them.

Once when a hymnal revision committee changed the word *worm* to the word *wretch*, pastor D. D. Holt got a call from an irate parishioner who declared, "I was born a worm, I am a worm, and I'll die a worm." Fanny Crosby might counter, "You may look like a worm, act like a worm, sound like a worm, but underneath your worminess is a beautiful chord waiting to vibrate."

Humility in the Bute Hall

*T*he Bute Hall was the grand room at Glasgow University, three floors high with fluted ceilings, stained glass windows, hardwood floors, and stone walls inside and out. It was the place where all big occasions were celebrated, occasions such as royal visits and inaugurations of Chancellors and Lord Rectors. It was an imposing room which could seat hundreds and whose acoustics allowed sounds to reverberate through it like thunder.

The most common uses for Bute Hall were degree examinations and degree conferring ceremonies, and I participated in both of these more than once. On two occasions I received important lessons in humility.

At the end of my second year as a student at Glasgow University, I "sat" the Hebrew examination, and it was taken in the Bute Hall. Now to appreciate fully the awe of the occasion, one needs to know a bit about the Scottish system of higher education. A student attends lectures, reads, writes, and takes class tests. But to receive a degree, examinations (not tests) are designed by external examiners, teachers and scholars from other universities in Great Britain and from Europe. These examiners are free to ask any question related to the field of study. Students write out their answers in "Blue Books," and they are mailed to the examiner who reads them and assigns them a grade: somewhat frightening for one's first examination. Even worse, the exam is given along with exams from all the faculties of the University. For example, when I sat for my Hebrew exam, only a handful of divinity students were present, but other students from the medical faculty, from the engineering and law faculties, from the arts faculties filled the massive room. The occasion and setting were daunting, to say the least.

The exam, itself, was even more daunting. Not that I was not prepared, I was. I knew my vocabulary, the sparse rules of grammar of biblical Hebrew, and I had studied in great detail the exegetical works on the books of The Old Testament. In our classes, we had studied each book with masoretic vowels added and with variant possible readings. We had even practiced "sight translations" of unfamiliar passages. I was a bit frightened, but prepared. Then, Professor Mullo-Weir, our Old Testament Professor and exam monitor, approached the five of us taking the exam. He had for each of us a complete copy of the Hebrew scriptures. Each copy was ten inches thick and must have weighed fifteen pounds. I had never seen a complete Hebrew Bible before. In our classes, we had worked on each "book" of the Bible using separate texts. This tome was massive, black, musty, ancient. Still, I reasoned, it has the same content as all the "little books" which I had studied. Not to worry.

I turned over my exam and read the first question. "Translate, with exegetical remarks, Ruth 3:6-14." Good, I really knew Ruth. I opened my examination edition of the Bible and proceeded to look for the Book of Ruth. I could not find it. Minutes passed as I continued to search for this short book. Then I remembered that in the Christian Bible, Ruth was placed among the "historical books," following Judges and before Samuel and Kings, but in the Hebrew scriptures, Ruth was considered a part of the "wisdom" literature. Moreover, the Hebrew Bible is read from back to front, and worst of all in Hebrew (without vowels) the entire book was only one and one-half pages long. Now it was time to worry. Finding one page among hundreds without an index, table of contents, or a familiar order was like looking for the proverbial needle in a haystack. After twenty minutes of futile searching, I was in a state of panic.

I raised my hand (we were not permitted to leave our seats), and from the elevated stage area where the

exam proctors for all the faculties sat came the sound of
Professor Mullo-Weir's high-pitched voice. "Yes, Mr.
Warren?" Up came the heads of examinees pouring over
their medical questions, their engineering problems, their
Latin translations, their mathematical equations. Their
eyes first focused on my professor and then followed his
gaze until they came to rest on my perspiring brow. In an
embarrassed voice I said, "Professor Mullo-Weir, my copy of
the Bible does not have a Book of Ruth in it." This elicited
from the assembled students first silent wondering, then a
few snickers, and finally outright guffaws. But from an
equally embarrassed Professor of Semitic Languages there
was nothing except charity and helpfulness. He walked to
the table where the Bibles were stacked, picked up one,
turned to the Book of Ruth, handed it to me and said with
his characteristic stutter, "Some of these old books have a
few pages missing." Saved by grace or at least by a graceful
person.

About a year later, I found myself again in the Bute
Hall, this time for a happier occasion. I was to receive my
Bachelor of Divinity degree. Only two of us were to receive
this degree, Peter Barrow, an Englishman who was soon to
immigrate to Canada, and me. Of course there were many
other degrees being conferred upon students from other
faculties, and Bute Hall was alive with friends and families
of the graduates. Members of the university were present,

lavishly clad with the trappings of their accomplishments. Professorial gowns of crimson and purple interspersed with the traditional black and hoods of every color imaginable (some even trimmed with fur) bore eloquent witness to the festive but serious nature of the event.

The highlight for each graduating student occurred when his or her name was read aloud by the Clerk of the University Senate and the student approached the front of the Hall to knell before the Chancellor. There the student handed his hood to the beadle and leaned toward the Chancellor, Sir Hector Hetherington. Sir Hector touched the student's head with an ancient Erasmus hat and intoned some serious sounding Latin phrases. Then the student arose, and the beadle placed the student's now-official hood around his neck. What an awesome occasion! One truly felt part of a history going back to the fifteenth century.

With pride of accomplishment and anticipation of this rite of passage, I lined up behind Peter, and we approached the Chancellor's chair. Peter knelt, and Sir Hector touched his head with that venerable hat, saying *"Te Sacrae Theologiae Bacculaureum creamus."* Peter arose, and I took my turn to kneel. I felt the hat graze my head, and I heard Sir Hector say, "Et tu."

I looked up with amazement and disappointment. *Et tu*? I thought. *Just an* et tu*? What happened to all those wonderful Latin phrases that bespoke the glory of learning and accomplishment? Could *et tu* capture all the work, pleasure, searching, and finding that had taken place in the past three years? Was I just an "et tu?" Were not my studies, my thoughts, my accomplishments distinct from all others? I confess that I felt more than let down, almost put down.

To this day I have mixed feelings about my Bute Hall experiences. I can laugh at my embarrassment in searching for the Book of Ruth, and can joke about my *et tu-ness*. But I ponder lessons regarding embarrassment, disappointment, and humility. From the Ruth episode I learned that no matter how well prepared I may be, I still need graceful help. From the graduation ceremony I learned that *et tu* may not be so bad, if our "me too-ness" places us in a venerable history, in a marvelous tradition, or among a "great cloud of witnesses."

"There Is a Place for Us"

*R*OTC at Duke University was spit and polish. If an exercise didn't come off like clockwork—if every cadet didn't come on line at exactly the right moment—well, there was "hell to pay." Perhaps the demand for precision was the reason that graduation in 1956 was both embarrassing and hilarious.

Earlier in the day, thirty of us were commissioned as second lieutenants in the United States Air Force. In a solemn ceremony, shining gold bars were pinned on our uniforms by parents and sweethearts. Then we marched in line with our fellow graduation candidates into a standing-room-only field house to receive our diplomas. In inviolate tradition, thirty special seats had been reserved for us.

Once we had received our degrees, we shirttail officers shucked our caps and robes to display our uniforms and bars and marched together to our reserved area. An officer snapped, "Seats," and we smartly followed his order. All of us, that is, save poor Fred Watkins. An interloper was occupying Fred's seat. As Fred continued to stand, titters—then uproarious laughter—filled the auditorium. After an eternity, the invader retreated and Fred took command of his rightful spot.

The foul-up, marring the dignity of my cherished day, burned itself into my psyche. Even now, I fear there won't be a place for me whether at a banquet, in a choir loft, or at a play. So, I'm always ready to depart the house early, and I pester family and friends with my nudges.

Maybe it's my need of a place for me that makes the lyrics of "Somewhere" from *West Side Story* so hauntingly appealing. Among special places, my foremost need is a home. In *The Wizard of Oz* that was Dorothy's sentiment after she was swept out of Kansas. We assume that homeplaces are important to everyone when we ask a new acquaintance, "Where do you live?" or "Where are you from?" It's a good icebreaker because as a rule the stranger can give a fond response.

"Footloose and fancy free" sounds appealing, but I can't relish that release without knowing I have a home base to which I will return. And if I feel queasy while traveling, I'm alarmed over the possibility that I'll grow ill in strange surroundings. When I'm sick, I want my family and familiar bed, couch, and bathroom.

Another appeal of home is that it's a place where I can be real. To be accepted, I don't have to shave or dress up or even be unfailingly cordial.

In addition to our "nests," we require insignificant retreats and stopovers on our life-journey. Remember when Brer Bear caught Brer Rabbit, and the captive began speaking beguilingly of his secret Laughing Place? The bear coerces the rabbit to take him there, but the surprise destination is a bee tree. The bees attack Brer Bear, and while he hops about in pain, Brer Rabbit laughs and laughs. I too need a laughing place. (I acknowledge that my place of mirth may not be a spot where you would get your jollies.)

I also need a Crying Place. During my childhood, when things went wrong I retreated to my tiny room upstairs in our farmhouse. There, I could weep unashamedly. And when it rained, I felt snug listening to my radio and the clatter on the tin roof. A few years later, I would spend my solitude in this retreat pondering the meaning of life and wondering about my future.

Goal-oriented as we are, we also need to envision a life's journey destination. Some of us will have "arrived" when we gain entrance to the executive dining suite. Or the promised land may be a second home on a lake or in the mountains.

Places hold special sway in the Bible. The localities where God spoke to the prophets are famous, and sites of terrible transgressions are doomed to notoriety. Simple places are nonetheless celebrated because Jesus lived, visited, or found retreat in them.

As I write this, I am aware that not everyone has a home. Some people do not even have access to a laughing place or a decent place to cry. Nor can they with assurance envision a meaningful destination. Perhaps what the world needs most are sharing places.

She Was Always There for Me

*M*y mother and father were like Mutt and Jeff. He was almost six feet tall; she was only four feet eleven. His easy stride was akin to a lope; she churned her short legs in quick, short steps like a frenetic bantam hen chasing bugs for her brood. Dad spoke quietly and persuasively; Mother loved to gab about anything and everything—family happenings, neighborhood news, politics, the world outlook, and her "other" families who had come to seem quite real as she listened to *Stella Dallas*, *Backstage Wife*, and *Ma Perkins*. My mother was surrounded by music as she hummed or sang hymns while she worked or as she listened to the radio while she rested for a spell. My dad, when and if he became aware of music, might absently drum his fingers to the beat. My father was a pragmatist; Mother was an idealist and dreamer.

Ostensibly Dad was head of our family, but it was Mother who set the tone and agenda, regulated our comings and goings, prodded and pleaded. Having reared one family—her five younger brothers and sisters—she was already an accomplished parent when

Betty and I came along. Mother had learned the power of positive reinforcement, but she also knew how to keep us in line: "Betty Ann Warren!" or "James Ivey Warren Junior!" When we heard our middle names called, we knew Mother was deadly serious about something we had done or had left undone. That "Junior" was the most deflating sound in the English language.

Just as my young life was surrounded by music, it also reverberated with talking and laughter. Some O'Briant long before my mother, Minnie, had kissed the Blarney stone and infected the family with the gift of gab for generations yet to come. All the O'Briants were talkers. Aunt Mary converted otherwise mundane events into hilarious comedies. My favorite was how the family dog became ensnarled in a garment hanging on the clothesline, broke the wire, and dumped the week's wash, bleach-whitened sheets and all, into mud. Aunt Mary's philosophy was, don't take life too seriously—even a mischievous dog can be as amusing as it is troublesome. I didn't know the term then, but Aunt Mary was a *satirist.*

Uncle R. M. had a joke to fit any conversation, and a few off-color gags that didn't fit but were awfully funny. His spontaneity was akin to psychiatrists' exercises in word association. He spoke softly, requiring his listeners to lean toward him. I don't know if this was contrived, but nowadays some experts recommend the ploy as a way to control one's listeners.

Aunt Ruby, Aunt Musette, and Uncle John conversed about everybody in Person County past and present, those with pedigrees

and those of dubious origin. A paucity of facts never discouraged
discussion. They were masters at making idiosyncrasies come alive.

In a weekly ritual, Aunt Musette, a trained cosmetologist,
came to our house to "fix" the hair of her three sisters, periodically
giving them a Toni permanent. During these three-hour evening
sessions, there wasn't one moment of silence. Often there was a
clamor as each sister strove to gain the floor to "speak my piece."
We children weren't admitted into the noisy beauty parlor, but from
the adjoining room we heard every word, every gasp, every snicker.

There were times when I thought my mother too directive
and overstrict, but these feelings have faded in importance. My
enduring sense of my mother resides in her gifts to me: idealism,
appreciation for family and friends, communication skills, love of
music, fascination with human behavior, and valuing each and every
day. But the greatest gift—she was always there!

Mother left her job in a department store to be with Betty
and me full time. When we departed for school each morning, she
saw us to the door to be sure we had everything we would need. If
we were in a play, sang in a chorus, received an award, she was
there. She held the book for spelling practice and Spanish
vocabulary checks. Mother gave our lives stability and security.
Beyond being there, mother was there *for* us.

I'm writing this on Christmas Day, the first Christmas Day
of my adult life when I did not visit, phone, or write Mother. She
died just a few months ago. There is a void in my life. For several
years, our roles were reversed. It was *I* who had advised *her*,

expressed concern over her health, tried to lift her spirits. Every Saturday I called whether or not there was anything of significance for us to discuss. We might talk about the Duke basketball team, the change of seasons, how some relative was getting along. And until this moment, I have presumed that I called because *I* wanted to be there for *her*. I was wrong. As in previous years, my mother was there for me. And now I miss her dreadfully. I don't know whether or not Mother was familiar with Carole King's song, "You've Got a Friend," but her whole being said to me that she was on my side, that if I called out to her she would come running. Her life sang out, "I'll be there."

Extended Family, Extended Blessings

I had a large extended family, although as a boy I never heard the term; indeed, I don't think it had yet been coined. All I knew was I was kin to half the people in Person County.

Granddaddy O'Briant, the patriarch, lived with us (my mother, dad, sister, and me). Well, technically we lived with him—it was his house. His wife had died, leaving him with four daughters and two sons. My mom, the eldest, became a mother to her siblings, the youngest only a toddler. When the brood grew up and flew the nest, she continued to keep house for her father and her husband—and eventually my sister, Betty, and me.

I said Mom's siblings flew the nest, but they didn't fly far. Mother's sisters, Mary and Ruby, had homes on land adjoining the "home place." Mother's brother, R. M., lived only a mile down the road and raised palomino horses in a pasture between our house and his. Mother's other brother, John, lived with us until I was thirteen. Only the youngest sister, Musette, "moved away"—three miles south—to Roxboro.

My sister and I never had reason to be lonesome. We had each other and seven cousins—Mac, Peggy, Sybil, Jean, Patsy, Buddy, and Linda—all within hollering distance. We played together (football, baseball, capture the flag, mumble peg, tops, marbles) like siblings, and we scrapped like siblings. My fondest memory is riding Mac's big, brakeless bicycle. The only way I could stop was to quit pedaling, head for a tree, and "parachute" just before the collision.

From my cousins, aunts, and uncles, I learned a lot: how to lead and persuade, scheme and build alliances, share and compromise, lose and regroup. But Granddaddy O'Briant was my primary example and mentor. He ran a general merchandise store near the main entrance of the velvet mill. The store, constructed of timber cut on the site, was small in the beginning, but as the mill grew and began operating three shifts, Granddaddy added a diner and butcher's shop. You walked back through the store on wood floors that were lightly oiled to control dust and came to the pot-bellied stove, and beyond it—a pool table! For farmers and townspeople alike, this was the community's recreation center, and Granddaddy let one and all play for free. My mother disapproved of this activity: "Unsavory people hang around pool halls, you know." But each Christmas, she joined the festivities when the table served as distribution center for the O'Briant clan's gifts.

To walk to and from work, Granddaddy cut across the pasture on a path lined with saplings I had blazed with Mac's runaway bicycle. Because my grandfather carried large sums of money, he toted a pistol. My mother disapproved of firearms and feared that the revolver, if brandished, would get her father shot, and so she removed the cartridges without his ever suspecting the gun was impotent. The weapon nevertheless gave Granddaddy the sense of security that he needed.

Every evening, Grandaddy's sitting room served our immediate family as a den, and oftentimes the extended family joined us. We gathered around the radio to listen to music ranging from the semiclassical *Firestone Hour* to the *Grand Ole Opry*. In this room also was stationed the piano around which we gathered for sing-alongs. Aunt Mary played the piano by ear and Uncle R. M. accompanied her on the guitar. Granddaddy had a sweet tenor voice which earlier had lent itself to gospel quartets. Our home resounded with hymns, and surrounded by these dear people, I felt as worshipful as I ever did in church.

Because I thought that everything my Granddaddy O'Briant did was wonderful, I'd stand beside him at our family sings. Once my voice matured I too became a tenor. I sang with my high school glee club, our church choir, and later with the Duke University Glee Club, and Chapel Choir. I treasure a picture of David Hartman ("Good Morning America") and me as members of the Duke quartet. In another area, the fact that my grandfather had been a pretty good baseball player heightened my pride as a young pitcher.

In high school, my greatest joy came from public speaking. My teacher and coach was Mrs. Mildred Nichols, a legend in the county, who had taught my mother before me. For decades, her students had ranked high in state speech contests, and I myself won several. My senior year, my best friend, Hunter Tillman, and I won the Aycock Cup in the state debating competition.

I was editor of the annual and an officer in the student government. I sang with the school band, dated the homecoming queen, and made straight A's. I had a lot going for me, but looking back I suspect I was at times cocky. Granddaddy O'Briant was aware of this, and one day he quietly and lovingly slipped a bridle over my pride. "Jimmy," he said, "every man to whom much is given, of him will much be required" (Luke 12: 48).

From his tone, I sensed that the verse was a rebuke, and it stung. But because I regarded my successes as accomplishments rather than as gifts, the import of my grandfather's counsel didn't hit me full force until years later. Now I recognize that I was indebted to good genes and to supportive parents, relatives (Granddaddy O'Briant!), teachers, and friends.

Often I think about grandfather's pool table; he could have charged his neighbors, but he offered it as a gift to the community. Mac's bicycle, decrepit as it was, gave great joy to all us cousins. And Miss Mildred's investment in young orators went far beyond the call of duty. I am blessed to have been born into a generous family and community.

Special Living: Marjorie and Martin Buber

"But it's a *special* day!"

I've heard these words a thousand times during my thirty plus years of marriage to Marjorie. The conversation goes like this:

"Jim, let's drive to Ithaca Tuesday."

"Marjorie! Do you remember how far it is?"

"Yes, but surely you want to be there for Heather's graduation. It's a special day!"

Or it's Halloween. Or Hilary's first prom. Whatever the occasion, Marjorie lights a candle under me, and I sputter. "I don't have the time." Or "We don't have the money." You can guess who prevails.

Many people have calendars packed with special days, each to be celebrated in special ways. Christmas means parties, decorations, gifts, cards, caroling, feasting—the whole nine yards (of ribbon). Churches too invest in special days. Advent is a time to look forward, Lent a time to look inward, Easter a time to look around. Liturgical vestment colors flash by us in a blur.

Special-day folk go wild over vacations. They endure the dreary winter by anticipating a breeze-swept beach. They slave away over stove or desk because, come June, somebody else will do the cooking, prepare the report. I was shocked at the degree to which vacation-itis infects Scotland. *Everyone*, rich or poor, takes a vacation—and vacation means *going* somewhere. Because of the climate, vacation usually means a change of rain—vacating one rainy place to take up residence in another. At least a vacation provides the rain of choice.

The stress (oops!) that people put on vacations was pounded into me when I became youth minister of Fairmont United Methodist Church in Raleigh, North Carolina. Our lively and bright youngsters supported thoughtful Sunday-night programs and year-round social projects. But the main focus, whether overtly or not, was always on the annual beach trip. To earn money, we washed cars, received pay for work and labor rendered, and sold everything from this to that. For months, we met and planned—housing, food, games, sharing time, worship. Our senior pastor, Fonnie Vereen, defined Methodist Youth Fellowship as a group of young people who spend half the year getting ready for the beach trip and the other half talking about how great it was.

Opposite the special-day people are the *every-day* people, for whom I serve as advocate. It was family influence that shaped me. We didn't make such a big deal of Christmas. Oh, we had a sumptuous meal and we exchanged gifts. (Remember Granddaddy

O'Briant's present-laden pool table?) But in honesty, I acknowledge that we *observed* special days more than celebrated them.

If I needed a new baseball glove, we bought one in spring or summer rather than wait for Christmas, which happens in the dead of winter. I went to only one circus and one state fair, but my dad and I went to local baseball games every week in season, and we journeyed often to the big cities of Durham and Danville. My dad's work dictated that he work throughout the summer, so we didn't sojourn in the mountains or loll on a beach. But that didn't mean that we as a family or I as an individual led lives devoid of fun. Our outlook was that *every* day is special.

Thinkers tend to fall within one or the other of these two contending groups. Historians credit progress either to pivotal events and charismatic leaders—or to evolutionary forces and gradual change. Some scientists are big-bang proponents, others offer creepy-crawly explanations.

Even (especially) theologians cling to either one or the other worldview. One of my favorite theologians is Martin Buber, best known for his seminal *I and Thou*. Buber does not believe in an overly sharp separation of God and the every day world. He says we must resist saying "Here God, there world." Rather we find God in the midst of daily, mundane activities. In doing this we "hallow the every day."

Ah, such idealism! How do we condition ourselves to recognize the holy amidst the ordinary, within the profane? What's uplifting about washing dishes? Elizabeth Barrett Browning testifies:

Earth's crammed with heaven,

And every common bush afire with God;

But only he who sees, takes off his shoes,

The rest sit round it and pluck blackberries.

Special-day people might argue that every-day people, welded to their daily lives, miss out on mountaintop experiences, while every-day folk can assert that their opposites are only living part time. Marjorie Warren has helped me appropriate the joy and meaning available in special occasions, and Martin Buber has helped me find the sacred in the midst of the every day. Marjorie is right—special days can come any day. Martin is right—every day can be special.

Fitting and Appropriate

*T*he first three grades were nice. The teachers were nice.
(They let us put our heads on our desks while they read
soothing stories.) Coloring with crayons was nice. Learning to read
and write was nice. Arithmetic was nice. Recess was *really* nice.

That's how it was supposed to be. The teachers' primary
goal was to have us love school and learning. Years later, I heard a
university professor observe, "All introductory courses are courses in
seduction. You want to seduce the student into falling in love with
the subject."

But fourth grade was hard! All the harder because we
dreaded it, having been frightened by its notoriety. The
subjects—geography, history, science, mathematics, and
English—were strange and demanding. The textbooks were thick
and devoid of the fun pictures that had brightened our early readers.
And our teacher, Miss Montague, was as stern as our older friends
had reported. Alas, the good old days were over.

Miss Montague, although her figure was appropriately

constrained, was Rubenesque, provoking snickers from some of the boys. But the rest of her was plain. Her clothing, shoes, and hairdo were "sensible," her gait determined, her speech decisive. To waste one's time on frivolous diversions was a sin; to illuminate and broaden one's mind was noble. Rarely did she indulge us with fun and games.

One thing about Miss Montague appealed to me: her patriotism. She kept us informed concerning current events, their causes and consequences. And she made history come alive. We galloped with Paul Revere, bushwhacked with Daniel Boone, applauded Patrick Henry. So it was not surprising that when our principal decided the school should start celebrating national anniversaries, he handed the assignment to Miss Montague. But I was shocked when she, in turn, appointed me to deliver an oration.

Miss Montague wrote the speech, but through countless rehearsals the words, gestures, and emphases became my own. I was so well coached that when the big occasion arrived I was at ease. Afterward, the principal told me I was as good as any preacher or politician he had ever heard. I was proud!

Strangely, the event that we commemorated and the text of my oration have vanished from my memory. All that I recall—and still hear reverberating through the auditorium—is the opening phrase: "It is fitting and appropriate that we pause today to . . . " (Did I go on autopilot after that?)

I now recognize that "fitting and appropriate" has a redundant ring. And I have learned that these authoritative words often shield actions that are unfair, unjust, immoral, and selfish. Yet, "fitting and appropriate" holds real promise. The words speak to our mores—folkways of central importance accepted without question and embodying the fundamental moral views of a group.

For example, when a member of a rural Southern community dies, fellow citizens "call on" the family. The women bring food and serve it not only to the bereaved, but also to guests. The menfolk sit on the porch or gather under trees, often with minimal conversation. What is fitting and appropriate carries the freight of caring, consoling, and pledging support. Being there can speak louder than words.

Another instance: A friend recalls dating a girl named Alla Kay. Whenever the couple left the house, her mother called to the daughter, "Alla Kay, remember who you are." In other words, see that your behavior is fitting and appropriate. And, my friend observes slyly, so far as he knows Alla Kay always lived up to that expectation.

Another example: In south Georgia I encountered an expression which was, to me, quaint. It was the use of "belong" in lieu of "ought," as in "I belong to be there." The implication is that an appropriate behavior belongs to (is inherent in) the person and situation.

Granted, "fitting and appropriate" are not always our ultimate criteria, for we must act out of our own sense of self in relation to God and neighbor. Still, a framework of acceptable behavior provides a ready reference for much of our daily living.

Dear, underappreciated Miss Montague! It is fitting and appropriate that I pause here to acknowledge the humanity that lay beneath her seeming stiff persona. I didn't know the word *humanist* then, but that's what she was. She was also an existentialist, calling us students to appreciate our own uniqueness, preserve our integrity, and seize our opportunities—whatever they might be. She gave generously of herself, instructing us by precept and example, and in the process we became better persons and better citizens.

Life's Semicolons: Pause But Don't Stop

Walter Towner was on a roll, and he wouldn't have stopped lecturing even if I had furiously waved my hands in front of him. We were supposed to be team teachers, but I felt more like his pupil. I was daunted by his self-assuredness and his seniority—he was in his seventies. Well, I too had important things to share with our class, so I squirmed, cleared my throat, and displayed my watch.

"Just one more sentence, Jim," Dr. Towner interposed. Instead, he ran on and on and on. When I thought he had come to a suitable stopping place, I eased out of my seat, but he grinned and said, "That wasn't a period, Jim, just a semicolon."

When Dr. Walter Towner and I became colleagues, I was a brand new college teacher eager to inform, persuade, entertain. On the day of which I speak, I felt cheated by Dr. Towner and the bell, and I left the classroom peeved. Yet, in honesty I had to acknowledge that my partner had said a lot. He spoke out of a wealth of experience and had a rare gift of insight which he accented from a treasury of apt sayings, such as "In this world, there's a whole lot more know-how than there is want-to."

Dr. Towner had twice come out of retirement to start new careers. He had been an engineer, pilot (World War I), pastor, and denominational executive. He was an authority in the field of education and an innovator of youth caravans and church-music fellowships. He continually honed our courses and devised new ways to promote them.

Dr. Towner was an optimist! Every problem had a solution—if only he (and I) would believe and seek. "See this angel on my shoulder?" he would tease. "He surely looks after me!"

He was, as I have suggested, persistent. This trait I admired whenever I judged the project at hand worthy of our unflagging effort; other times, his doggedness drove me crazy. Fellow faculty members likened his impact on colleagues and students to the drip, drip, drip of water on a prisoner's skull.

Had Walter Towner written a book on the art of living, he would have eshewed periods, or "full stops" as the British say. Instead, he would have employed commas and semicolons as platforms for plunging on. His pursuit of knowledge and understanding was insatiable, and no area of inquiry was sacrosanct. "As I get older," he said, "I find that I believe less, but I believe it more deeply."

Dr. Towner died in 1993, at the age of ninety-seven.

Sometimes when I'm perplexed, weary, and ready to surrender, I think of my buoyant friend and mentor and his meandering expositions that moved relentlessly toward truth and light, refusing to be flagged by either a grammatically correct period or an impatient young coteacher. If, infrequently he paused, it was only to insert a comma or semicolon to indicate a fresh breath for pursuing a fresh thought.

Real love and sincere hope are like that. They aren't easily derailed; instead, they either plow straight through or they back up and go around the obstacle. Their transforming power triumphs.

To List or Not To List

*R*abbi Marc Gellman has written a witty and wise book called *Does God Have a Big Toe?* Each chapter is a contemporary *midrash* (interpretation of a biblical text). I love the one entitled "No Lists on the Sabbath," which suggests that Eden was not the perfect place we've assumed, and all because Adam was a list-maker.

Every day, Adam dipped his pen in berry juice and wrote out a chore list—what Girl Scouts call a "caper chart"—for the animals. (After all, God had given Adam dominion.) The elephants were assigned to stomp coconuts, the monkeys to gather bananas, and so forth. The animals felt unfairly burdened and asked God to fire their boss. "Wait for the Sabbath," God responded.

On the morning of the Sabbath, Adam began scribbling his chore list, but the berry ink instantly disappeared. He tried to trace the assignments in sand, but waves washed over them. Adam took his perplexity to God, who explained that the Sabbath was a day different from the other days. One distinction, there were to be no lists on the Sabbath!

I responded to the rabbi's story with glee. You see, there are two kinds of people (in addition to special-day and every-day). There are the list-makers (disciples of Adam), and there are the list-haters, of which I am one. I side with the animals: Lists are an abomination.

I have friends and colleagues who are indentured to lists of "Things to do today." They also maintain lists of birthdays and anniversaries. Many people carry little black books to prompt them concerning medical appointments, their children's school programs, committee meetings, tee-off times. Some take grocery lists so seriously they computerize them. And even we who hate lists and profess we're only concerned with the "big picture" may have somebody (a secretary or spouse, perhaps) who maintains notes that keep us on track. Our aloofness and unprepareness can allow others to dominate us; for example, when a committee is considering its next meeting date, we default and the list-makers pop out their calendars and suit their own convenience.

My twinges of inadequacy and guilt concerning lists were swept away by an unlikely teaching team, Don Welch and Andrew Strickland.

Don Welch is an educator with intuitive judgment and creative flair. I met him at Scarritt College following his teaching stints at Duke University Divinity School and Wofford College. At those institutions, Don's quick mind earned the respect of his colleagues, while his restless and searching spirit won the confidence of students. At Scarritt, he was that rarest of academicians, a rebellious administrator.

Scarritt had for almost a century trained effective Christian educators, church and community workers, missionaries, and deaconesses but now was tottering. Don's challenging and painful task was to renew the venerable institution or preach its funeral. His restructuring included personnel changes, financial economies, new programs, and new degrees. His forthright actions won mixed reviews; to some, he was a hatchet man, to others, a savior.

Don combined the grassroots wisdom of his native Kentucky with the urbanity of contemporary theological education. He spun yarns in the vivid language of master storytellers, inventing metaphors as he went. He once likened his faculty members to various fabrics. Bob O'Gorman, who had a touch of brogue and a devilish twinkle in his eye, was "smooth Irish linen." Wilma Jensen, a grand lady who could play the organ with the delicacy of a butterfly or with the power of a thunderstorm, was "lace."

But the wisdom that Don passed to me didn't arise out of his driving, Type A personality, which led him to overload on campus, professional, denominational, civic, and family responsibilities. Don suffered a heart attack and underwent surgery. A doctor counseled: "Make two lists. On one, list the things you *have* to do. On the other, the things you *want* to do. Schedule your life around these two lists and let the rest go."

Having observed the toll exacted by Don's compulsive nature, I reviewed my daily activities and discovered that I spent a lot of time and energy on activities that were neither necessary nor pleasing. I catered to people whose professed needs were of marginal importance. I listened to "ghost voices" that whispered "must," "ought," and "should." Enlightened, I adopted Don's prescription, and the result has been a happier, more productive, and healthier life.

Andrew Strickland, the other instrument of wisdom, is just a little boy. He's my three-year-old, lively, chatty grandson. During several days spent together, we entertained ourselves with bedtime stories and drives in the countryside. The amusement triggered a myriad of questions.

"Why do cows eat grass?"

"Why were there *seven* dwarfs?"

"Why do ducks quack so loud?"

Being a with-it grandfather, I attempted to answer Andrew's queries seriously and fully—and interminably.

"Ducks quack loudly so they can call to other ducks."

"Why do they want to do that?"

"To warn their friends that we are coming."

"Why do they warn them?"

"Because they are afraid of us."

Why, why, why?

Exhausting myself with explanations which nonetheless failed to satisfy my young companion, I hit upon alternative answers having a wonderful built-in finality: "Because they (he/she/it) *have* to." Or, "Because they (he/she/it) *want* to." Amazingly, Andrew found these answers satisfying.

Don and Andrew, two very different people. But each of them helped me with two of life's profound questions, What? and Why?

Cryptoquotes

*E*ach morning, "Cryptoquote" takes up nine square inches of the newspaper and ten minutes of my time. The game holds a message that has been obscured by the substitution of code letters for the real letters, and the idea is to figure out what the cryptographer had in mind. It's an entertaining way to begin one's day. And for those who grew up on secret messages planted by the Lone Ranger or Tom Mix or Jack Armstrong (the All-American Boy), it's an innocent way to slip back into one's childhood, but with the benefit of adult knowledge and skills.

The quotes are sometimes humorous, sometimes insightful, sometimes both. Here are samples:

"We cannot control the evil tongues of others; but a good life enables us to disregard them." (Cato)

"The amount of sleep required by the average person is just five minutes more." (Anonymous)

"Man endures pain as an undeserved punishment; woman

accepts it as a natural heritage." (Anonymous)

Occasionally, I say "Now, that's insightful!" (How else can I justify spending ten minutes uncovering the quote? Another reward is the sense of camaraderie with a legion of fellow cryptographers and sages!) In my view, an insightful statement is one that is both true and well expressed; its appeal may lie more in its well-crafted, pithy language than in its originality of ideas. (The truth may be familiar to me, the expression of it novel.)

My favorite Cryptoquote was borrowed from Malcolm Forbes: "Education's purpose is to replace an empty mind with an open one." Statements about education catch my eye because I have spent practically all of my life either giving or receiving education: public school, college, seminary, junior college teacher, graduate school professor and dean, and director of a center for continuing education—approaching fifty years!

Midway into my teaching career, I became a little uneasy over never having taken an education course. Earlier I hadn't let it bother me because I had encountered many teachers long on technique and short on content, which I thought a bad trade-off. Now I wondered about my philosophy of education—if I had one.

My colleagues readily defined and articulated their philosophies. One "shook the foundations" of his students' experiences. He confronted fundamentalists with logical, historical, and literary problems with the Bible; meanwhile, he needled liberals with questions about the need for absolutes and consistencies. A second teacher, who stressed information, required voluminous reading and reporting. A third stressed practicality and filled her charges' days and nights with projects and field assignments. A fourth prodded his students to reflect, reflect, reflect on experiences and information.

Imagine the debates that ensued when I, as dean of the faculty, brought our academicians together for one of our periodic endeavors: "Redesign the Curriculum." My colleagues, studied and informed as they were, forcefully advocated their positions. My problem was, I liked it all. And my universal approach prevailed, not because I was dean, but because the others would not yield. Our final document contained something for everybody: It emphasized knowledge, skills, understanding, and appreciation. Of course, we never fully agreed about what should be fitted into these compartments.

I concluded that I did, indeed, have a philosophy of education—and a good one, largely based on what I had found to work. From guiding students in their field work, I learned the value of practical ministerial skills. From teaching theology, I pushed students to articulate tenets and values of their faith. Church history revealed the need to be rooted in one's heritage. Also, I delighted when students thought deeply about personal values and moral issues. I concluded that it wasn't my mission to produce disciples of Piaget or Tillich or Fletcher—to mold conservatives or liberals. Rather, my intended role was to see that the students formed their own decisions after reflecting upon and evaluating a broad base of information and experience. Besides, we were not, as some educators seemed to think, turning out finished products.

Empty minds need filling and closed minds need airing. These objectives have made my vocation challenging and fulfilling.

Miss Mildred and Stickability

*M*iss Mildred was short and stocky with a round, bespectacled face, and when she strode through the halls of Roxboro High School, she reminded me of an army tank. Few students ever learned that behind Miss Mildred's businesslike manner there lurked a keen sense of humor begging to be exercised. Corny jokes and raucous tales did not please her; her appetite was for anecdotes that revealed human nature. Subtleties that barely provoked a smile in most us could send her into spasms of laughter.

Miss Mildred had the difficult assignment of teaching senior English—including a considerable chunk of Shakespeare—to ninety rural kids who saw no practical value in *forsooths* and *prithees.* (Give them Erle Stanley Gardner and Erskine Caldwell.) To reassure herself that we hadn't slighted the bard, Miss Mildred gave us her famous one-hundred quotations test. With each quotation, we had to identify the play and the character, and give the context and meaning.

One day, passing Miss Mildred's open door, I heard a

chuckle and stopped for a closer look. She was grading papers, and by now her giggles had exploded into guffaws. Curious, I gave a little knock and went in to find tears rolling down the teacher's cheeks. Coyly, she dared to share the source of her mirth. Bill Bradshaw, our star basketball player, had taken a stab at the quotation "Lay on, Macduff, And damn'd be him that first cries, 'Hold, enough!'" (*Macbeth*, act 5, scene 7)

Bill's errant answer: "Lady Macduff, talking to her husband on her wedding night. This shows her strength of character."

Earlier, this same athlete had amused the class during yet another reluctant encounter with poetry, this from John Milton ("L'Allegro"). Miss Mildred was trying to draw from him the passage "Come, and trip it as ye go, On the light fantastic toe." In a hint, the teacher asked, "Bill, what do you say to a girl when you want to dance with her?" Bill, out of a vague recollection, said, "Come, trip with me."

Mildred Satterfield had taught for years before marrying Dr. Nichols, a physician, and the "Miss" endured (which wasn't unusual for married ladies in that place and time.) Because Dr. Nichols was as invested in his practice as Miss Mildred was in her teaching, some people wondered what they shared in common. I think it was their fondness for offbeat humor. I recall a Halloween when a coven of witches knocked on the Nichols' door intent on either enjoying a treat or inflicting a trick (perhaps overturning garbage cans or relocating porch furniture). The door opened and the couple presented themselves in green hospital scrub suits, Miss Mildred brandishing cotton swabs and rubbing alcohol as accompaniment to the doctor's flourishing offer of a hypodermic needle. There were no takers, and no tricks.

As I have mentioned earlier, Miss Mildred taught me public speaking for four years, and profitable years they were. I learned how to compose—and be composed. We had one of the strongest chapters of the National Forensic League, and we fledgling orators won many public speaking competitions far and wide. The art of speaking was for me what basketball was for Bill Bradshaw, and I developed self-confidence and self-esteem.

I cherish the prizes Miss Mildred afforded me, but her greatest gift—a gift of wisdom—came indirectly. At the end of each year, she presented medals, the most coveted being "Best Achievement." But Miss Mildred recognized that opportunities vary because native talent and home influences vary; consequently, some students began the race way back of the starting line. Thus her "Most Improved" award. And yet another prize, which didn't impress me then but now packs a lot of meaning—a medal inscribed "For Stickability."

I suppose achievement came rather easily for me since I had a large family cheering section. But what about those kids who came from environments deprived of money and education? Some were yoked to farm drudgery both before and after school, and even had to stay out of school during the planting and harvesting seasons. Many lacked a pat on the back, much less applause from the student body, and each year Miss Mildred provided a few of these youngsters a moment of acclamation. And know what? True to the fable of the hare and the tortoise, some of those slow starters have, in later life, proved themselves to be winners of the race.

To Thine Own Grass Be True

*I*t was a perfect Saturday for baseball. But it would also be a perfect day for cutting grass, and this troubled me. I merely toyed with my eggs.

"Dad," I blurted, "do we really have to mow the grass?"

A reproving "Yes, Son" came from behind the newspaper.

For a month my father and I had talked about that afternoon's game between our village, Ca-Vel, and our biggest rival, Longhurst. Now there was a hitch. After week-long rains that kept the lawn soggy, the sun was shining. Soon the grass would dry, and my dad and I would be slaving away. We couldn't possibly finish in time for the first pitch.

I was ten, and I had a great respect and affection for my father. He spent hours playing catch with me, and I had developed into a pretty fair pitcher for a kid. I had a "fast" ball, a round-house curve, and a pitch I glowingly called my "inside" curve that was supposed to break in on a right-handed batter.

Dad and I saw every home game, and we knew all the

players. Everybody knew everybody else in Ca-Vel. Our North Carolina village's name combined "Vel" (for velvet factory) with the initials of the owners, Collins and Aikman. Most of the players were mill employees. Robert Slaughter, kinsman of St. Louis Cardinal outfielder Enos Slaughter, could catapult a ball from deep center field to home plate. Sam Shotwell, another outfielder, had refused to let the loss of his right hand in combat in World War II relegate him to the sidelines. He batted, caught, and threw with his left hand. Upon snagging a fly, he shucked his glove, grasped the ball, and pegged it.

The field, which was on Grandfather O'Briant's property across the railroad tracks, was, in my young eyes, a grand one. The infield was hard, red clay, regularly smoothed by a tractor and drag provided by the velvet factory. For the Longhurst games, it seemed everybody in the county turned out. Packed behind the fence would be old codgers in overalls and straw hats, women in summer frocks, and children in playsuits. More importantly, all my friends would be there. For a nickel, we would have a frosty bottle of Coca-Cola from an ice-filled tub. The game was Ca-Vel's social event of the season.

I glared out the kitchen window at my nemesis, the lawn mower. It was the old motorless kind, with a reel of blades that rotated like the paddles of a stern-wheel boat. Routinely, rocks gapped the blades and sticks jammed them, and the machine fairly surrendered in the presence of overgrown grass. Our lot was practically a ranch, two acres! Surely, I reasoned, the ball game was more important than the appearance of our yard.

The newspaper came down. "Eat your breakfast," Dad urged. Then, seeing how disconsolate I was, "Cheer up, Jimmy. If we take turns and work hard, we can be at the game by the third inning."

About ten, Dad tested the grass and pronounced it mowable. Faced with a now-or-never crisis, I offered a compromise I had cooked up. It made sense to me. We would cut the front, whose importance I could appreciate since it faced Highway 501, the main thoroughfare. The back would wait. It was remote and ordinary—just a few trees and several out-buildings.

"Nobody ever sees it," I contended.

"But you and I see it, don't we, Son?" Dad rejoined.

My strategem rejected, we got that mower rolling. When we finished, Dad surveyed the back lawn and observed, "It looks pretty good." I hastily agreed. Then we rushed to the ball field, arriving in the third inning, as Dad had promised. Ca-Vel won!

Since then, I have studied the celebrated ethical systems of giants like Paul Ramsey, Reinhold Niebuhr, and Joseph Fletcher. I have debated the moral implications of civil rights marches, draft-card burnings, the Viet Nam war, and alternate lifestyles. I am familiar with many eloquent advocacies of self-worth and self-esteem, including Shakespeare's

> This above all: to thine own self be true,
> And it must follow, as the night the day,

Thou canst not then be false to any man.

(*Hamlet*, act 1, scene 3)

Still, whenever I'm tempted to decide an issue on the basis of what someone else might say or think—whenever I incline toward pushing aside my own importance and sense of values, it isn't these pronouncements that pull me up short. Much plainer words echo within me, my dad's "But you and I see it, don't we, Son?"

Epitaphs

*G*raveyards fascinate me. At least, old graveyards do. I like to wander among the headstones and read about the persons remembered. For example, there is a small but interesting cemetery in Nashville, Tennessee, full of grassy spots, winding paths, and old, weatherworn headstones. I recall two grave markers in particular. The tombstone of sea captain William Driver is adorned with graven flags, and the chiseled legend in the stone tells all visitors that he was the person who dubbed the United States flag, "Old Glory." A second gravestone marks the burial place of Nashville's first teacher, and it has a scene engraved upon it—the picture of a woman with several children seated at her feet.

Not long ago I was visiting the area where I was reared, Person County in north central North Carolina. Having a couple of free hours, I drove around the county and explored two church graveyards. The churches were those attended by my grandparents and several generations of their forebears. I read descriptions such as "beloved wife of . . . " or "infant daughter of . . .," and in my romantic wonderings I imagined those early settlers who came from Virginia and Pennsylvania to clear the land, establish farms, and create communities. I felt a sense of roots. This is where I came from, and these people played a part in making me who I am. Cemeteries and gravestones can provide thoughtful and sentimental settings.

Some gravestone inscriptions have even earned a degree of fame. Benjamin Franklin, whose chosen profession was book printing, has a epitaph that is at once appropriate, witty, and profound.

> The body of Benjamim Franklin, Printer,
> Like the covering of an old book, its contents
> torn out and stripped of its lettering and gilding,
> lies here, food for worms;
> But the work shall not be lost,
> it will (as he believed) appear once more,
> in a new and more elegant edition,
> revised, and corrected by the Author.

A New England graveyard contains an inscription that tells little about the deceased but provides a glowing advertisement for his widow.

> Sacred to the Memory of Mr. Jared Bates
> who Died Aug. the 6th 1800.

His Widow aged 24 who mourns as one who can be
comforted lives at 7 Elm Street this village
and possesses every qualification for a Good Wife.

Epitaphing may be a source of wisdom and self-understanding. Like many "with it" people of the 1970's, I became interested in transactional analysis and its textbook *I'm O.K., You're O.K.* One of the techniques we employed to help a person ascertain who he or she wanted to become was to ask, "What would you like to have written on your gravestone?" Some answers revealed an appreciation for diligence ("She always did her best.") Some showed a life open to change and improvement ("Still growing.") A friend of mine who was an avid fox hunter demonstrated wit and hope when he suggested his epitaph should be the phrase used when the fox escapes the hounds and hunters—"Gone to ground."

Let me propose an epitaph that tells much about one of my most admired colleagues and one of my favorite institutions. This will be a living epitaph, for both are very much alive. The man is Lawrence Hay and the institution is Scarritt College. Lawrence Hay was a professor of biblical studies for more than twenty years. His students always called him Dr. Hay, for he was respected by all and even feared by a few, enjoying the reputation of a strict, demanding teacher. Late papers were unheard of, and no one in his or her right mind would try to bluff Dr. Hay. For awhile, I too called him Dr. Hay, although we were faculty colleagues and he was but a few years older than I. Somehow I came across as "Jim" or "James I."

while his persona was "Dr. Hay." His lectures were riveting, his strong advocacy of the historical-critical approach to biblical studies often "shook the foundations" of his students' beliefs. They would leave his classes with worrisome questioning of their faith and sincere appreciation for Dr. Hay's rigorous scholarship. Between classes Lawrence Hay could be found almost every day sitting in the quadrangle discussing biblical theology with interested students. He was a teacher who cared deeply that his students develop a theologically and biblically grounded faith.

Lawrence Hay's academic training and classroom skills qualified him to teach at any of the world's "great" universities or seminaries, but things did not work out that way. While he was completing his Ph.D. studies at Vanderbilt University, he taught part time at tiny Scarritt College, just across the street. Dr. D. D. Holt, President of Scarritt College, recognized Dr. Hay's abilities, so when Vanderbilt awarded him his degree, President Holt phoned Dr. Hay to offer him a full-time position. Like Nathanael (John 1:47) Lawrence Hay is a man in whom there is no guile. He immediately said *yes* to the offer, but his wife who was overhearing the conversation advised, "Don't say *yes* so quickly. Ask what it will pay, and tell him you will think about it. Play a little hard to get." So, Lawrence Hay resumed his conversation with President Holt and said, "How much does it pay?" Then he paused to hear the answer. "Well, I'll have to think about it and let you know in a few days." Then, typical of his what-you-see-is-what-you-get character he added, "But, I'll probably take it."

Take it he did, and Lawrence Hay spent his entire academic career teaching at Scarritt College. Scarritt was never considered in the broad spectrum to be a "great" university or seminary. The largest enrollment it ever enjoyed was just over 200. To my knowledge, none of its graduates ever became a United States President or a United States Senator or a Wall Street success. Most of Scarritt's graduates went to serve as missionaries in developing countries or as community workers in rural and urban centers, or as church educators and musicians in local churches. But if I correctly understand Jesus when he pointed out to his followers that to be great is to serve, then Scarritt College and its graduates participate in true greatness.

In the fall of 1993 Scarritt College (now the Scarritt-Bennett Center) celebrated one hundred years of training and educating persons for Christian service. Many of Scarritt's former faculty members were present for the occasion, and each was given a brief time to share what was happening in his/her life, to recall some significant moment while at Scarritt, or just to offer greetings to the assembled graduates and church dignitaries. When it came Lawrence Hay's turn to speak, he said, "All I ever wanted to do was earn my degree and teach at a great college. And I did."

Now, that's an epitaph!

Dr. James I. Warren is Director of The Intentional Growth Center (an agency of the United Methodist Church) in Lake Junaluska, North Carolina. Prior to this position he was Cadwallader Professor of Global Evangelism and the Mission of the Church at Scarritt Graduate School in Nashville, Tennessee.

The author is a native of North Carolina and has pastored United Methodist churches in North Carolina and Tennessee. He has served as preacher/teacher and retreat leader for annual conferences, local churches in Florida, Alabama, Tennessee, Virginia, North Carolina and South Carolina, and at various seminaries. He holds degrees from Duke University (A.B.) in North Carolina and Glasgow University (B.D. and Ph.D) in Scotland.

Among Dr. Warren's interests and hobbies are tennis, hymnology, and Christian spirituality. He is the author of *O For a Thousand Tongues: The History, Nature, and Influence of Music in the Methodist Tradition*. He is married to Marjorie, a noted tartan authority and handweaver, and they have three children.